MW01075822

Excommunication
and the
Catholic Church

Straight Answers to Tough Questions

Edward N. Peters, J.D., J.C.D.

Foreword by Most Rev. Thomas J. Paprocki, D.D., S.T.L, J.D., J.C.D.,
Auxiliary Bishop of Chicago

ASCENSION PRESS

West Chester, Pennsylvania

Scripture verses contained herein are from the Catholic Edition of the
Revised Standard Version of the Bible, copyright 1965, 1966 by the Division
of Christian Education of the National Council of the Churches of Christ in the
United States of America. Used by permission. All rights reserved.

Ascension Press
Post Office Box 1990
West Chester, PA 19380
Orders: (800) 376-0520
www.ascensionpress.com

Cover design: Kinsey Caruth

Printed in the United States of America

ISBN-10: 1-932645-45-4
ISBN-13: 978-1-932645-45-3

*In gratitude to those who build up the Body of Christ,
and in petition for the grace to emulate them more closely.*

Contents

Acknowledgments vii

Foreword ix
by Most Reverend Thomas J. Paprocki, D.D., S.T.L., J.D., J.C.D.,
Auxiliary Bishop of Chicago

Introduction xiii

Questions & Answers 1

Glossary of Terms 55

Index 59

Index of Canons Cited 63

About the Author 65

Acknowledgments

The further I advance in life, the more I realize the impossibility of acknowledging all those who have shared with me their erudition, insights, patience, and basic kindness. Ten years ago, for example, I asked one Fr. Thomas Paprocki, J.D., J.C.D., how I could get a copy of his dissertation on administrative justice in the Church. To my surprise he sent me his own spare copy which I promptly and gratefully read. Now, Bishop Paprocki has provided just the right foreword to my own book. All my life I have been blessed by such considerate acts; I only pray to be the best steward I can of such generosity.

May I add, though, that this particular book owes a considerable debt to people with their finger on the pulse of the Catholic print and electronic media, men such as Matthew Pinto at Ascension Press, who knew all along that this book needed to be written. Similarly, Catholic radio hosts such as Jerry Usher, Al Kresta, and Drew Mariani gave me several opportunities to hear directly and ponder the questions that modern Catholics are asking about the ancient topic of excommunication. After each interview, I went back to my sources in search of new and better ways to address the issues raised by their listeners, and I think each time I did that, I came away a little better canon lawyer. Thus, to each of these gentlemen, too, I am very grateful.

Foreword

"Excommunication" is one of the most highly-charged and feared words connected with the Catholic faith. It is also one of the most misunderstood. Many people incorrectly believe that a person who has been excommunicated has been "kicked out" of the Catholic Church. They may also think that this is a permanent and irreversible punishment. The penalty may be viewed as harsh, lacking in charity, even un-Christian.

In this book, *Excommunication and the Catholic Church*, Dr. Edward Peters sets the record straight and answers a variety of questions about the ecclesiastical sanction known as "excommunication." This type of analysis is very needed and timely.

During the revision of canon law which took several years to complete following the conclusion of the Second Vatican Council in 1965, and which culminated in the publication of the revised *Code of Canon Law* in 1983, there were many voices, including some bishops and canon lawyers, who were calling for the complete abolition of all penalties in canon law. Ideally, it was thought, everyone would conform to the law voluntarily out of love for Christ and His Church. Realistically, however, not everyone conforms easily to the ideal. Thus, while coercive penalties were retained as necessary for maintaining proper order in any society, one of the ten principles for the revision of the

Code of Canon Law was that penalties should be kept to a minimum.

Excommunication belongs to the genus of sanctions known as censures, in contrast to expiatory penalties. Expiatory penalties (canon 1336) punish the offender for a prescribed time or an indefinite time and seek to remedy the damage or injustice done to societal values by the offense and to deter others from engaging in similar wrongdoing. In contrast, censures are considered to be "medicinal penalties" (canon 1312, §1, 1º), which means that they seek to persuade the offender to cease the wrongful behavior and reintegrate the person into the life of the ecclesial community. As such, censures are lifted when the offender "withdraws from contumacy," i.e., from engaging in the wrongful behavior and making suitable reparation for damages, if necessary (see canons 1347 and 1358).

Properly understood in this way as a medicinal penalty, excommunication certainly does not expel the person from the Catholic Church, but simply forbids the excommunicated person from engaging in certain activities (listed in canon 1331) in the life of the Church until the offender reforms and ceases from the offense. Once this happens, the person is to be restored to the fullness of participation in the life of the Church. Although the remission of the censure pertains to the competent authority to determine whether the person has actually withdrawn from contumacy, in a sense the offender holds in his or her own hand the key to the release from the censure. If the wrongful behavior ceases and any necessary reparation or restitution is made, the excommunication will be lifted; if not, it continues.

Thus, some people may be excommunicated for only a short time. For others, the excommunication may never be lifted if they do not repent and change their ways. Church history over the past two millennia provides many examples of both, some of them described in this book by Dr. Peters. For example, King Henry VIII was excommunicated for defying the Pope and declaring himself to be head of the church of England (today called the Anglican Church, except in the United States, where it is known as the Episcopal Church due to the desire of the American revolutionaries to disassociate themselves from identity with England). Henry VIII never "withdrew from contumacy" and hence died excommunicated. In contrast, the racist segregationist Leander Perez was excommunicated by New Orleans Archbishop Joseph Rummel in 1962, but since Perez repented before his death in 1969, he died as a Catholic in good standing with the Church. This is the outcome that the Church seeks and fervently desires.

Seen in this way, a censure such as excommunication is not at all vindictive, but may be seen as a sort of "tough love," just as loving parents discipline their children to teach them the difference between right and wrong. In fact, it would be most unloving to allow someone to persist in their wrongdoing without pointing out the fault. Jesus spoke about fraternal correction (Matthew 18:15-17) and St. Paul wrote that "love is the fulfillment of the law" (Romans 13:10). My own Episcopal motto reflects this: Lex Cordis Caritas, that is, the Law of the Heart is Love.

Dr. Peters has provided his readers with an excellent description of the Church's loving remedy known as excommunication, by which all the Christian faithful may be formed into the one holy, Catholic and apostolic Church as the loving Bride of Christ (Ephesians 5:22-33).

—Most Reverend Thomas J. Paprocki, S.T.L., J.D., J.C.D.
Auxiliary Bishop of Chicago,
Adjunct Professor of Law,
Loyola University Chicago School of Law

Introduction

Probably no word in Catholic life provokes more misunderstanding than "excommunication." The range of reactions this term has engendered over the centuries is startling. For some, excommunication conjures up images of secret tribunals pronouncing eternal damnation on cowering heretics; for others, excommunication is tantamount to a badge of honor earned by individuals of noble conscience and steady nerves. In reality, neither image is correct.

Excommunication has very ancient roots in ecclesiastical life, yet it remains a living part of modern ecclesiastical law. Today, after a generation or so of being out of the public eye, excommunication is once again making the news. It is increasingly important, therefore, that the public, both Catholic and otherwise, has a clear grasp of both what is and what is not entailed in excommunication.

This book provides a basic survey of the theology, canon law, and history of excommunication. It explains how, for example, excommunication can simultaneously be the Church's most severe penalty and yet also serve as the strongest *medicinal* response she has to certain forms of offending behavior. It sets out who has authority to pronounce excommunications and who has authority to lift them. We will ask what the consequences are, in this life and the next, for those who fall under excommunication, and we will discuss what the responsibilities are of the rest of the faithful in regard to those excommunicated. Finally, without overloading these pages with technical citations, we will offer succinct references to the *Code of Canon Law* and other reliable resources that will enable readers to verify the information offered here or at least to understand what supports the opinions presented herein.

As more and more people discover—or rediscover, as the case may be—the importance of being in communion with the Catholic Church, more questions will naturally arise about the state of being "ex-communicated" from the Church. It is my hope that this small work will enable readers not only to understand what excommunication means, but, along the way, to appreciate better what a grace it is to be a member of the Mystical Body of Christ.

—Edward N. Peters, J.D., J.C.D.
August 22, 2006

Questions & Answers

1. What is excommunication?

Excommunication is the most serious punishment the Church can impose on one of its members. It is two things:

- An ecclesiastical (that is, Church-authorized) penalty contained in the *Code of Canon Law* which can be imposed only for certain offenses, and then only in accord with certain procedures;

- A form of public stigma that attaches to certain persons who engage in actions or advocate positions that the Church condemns as being especially reprehensible. As a result of these actions, the Church responds in severe form.

2. *Canon law?* What's that all about?

Canon law is the main set of rules—or *canons*—by which the Catholic Church operates. Most of the important regulations of canon law can be found between the covers of a single book, the *Code of Canon Law*, most recently issued in 1983, replacing the former code of 1917. It is available in numerous modern translations from its official Latin text.

The *Code of Canon Law* contains many fascinating provisions, some of which reach back to the very earliest days of the Church. It affects a wide variety of religious, moral, and administrative areas in ecclesiastical life. Some canons reflect fundamental principles derived from divine or natural law, but most are of "human" origin in that Church leaders, over the centuries, have developed certain ways of organizing the conduct of the Church's earthly mission, and these are reflected in canon law.

Specifically for our topic, the majority of the canons on excommunication are found in Book VI of the 1983 Code, called "Sanctions in the Church." In these pages, citations to canon numbers are provided for most answers so that readers can see how a particular answer is rooted in canon law. By the way, Eastern Catholics (for example, Maronite or Chaldean rite Catholics) have their own code of canon law that was issued in 1990. Here, though, we will be focusing on canons that apply only to *Roman* Catholics.

3.   Could you give me a quick history of canon law?

The history of canon law is long and complex. The quick overview given below might stimulate your interest in reading more about it.

Any community that wants to survive and remain cohesive needs law. So it is not surprising that, from very early on, the Christian community established laws. We can see this reflected in the New Testament, such as when Our Lord prohibited divorce and remarriage for His followers (Matthew 19:9). As Christianity spread, these laws developed in various ways. The first *ecumenical* (that is, general) council, Nicaea (A.D. 325), and subsequent councils established rules called "canons." In addition, the Church fathers, Roman law, and efforts to provide solutions for local problems all played a role in developing ecclesiastical law.

After the collapse of the Roman Empire, Church law played a significant role in the attempt to restore civilization. In the Middle Ages, Pope Gregory VII used law to consolidate the Church as an institution independent of the state. Another major development occurred around 1141 with Gratian's work in systematizing the canons. In the sixteenth century, the Council of Trent, responding to the Protestant Reformation, used canon law as a vehicle of reform. In the late 19th century, the First Vatican Council intended—but did not succeed in—revising canon law. Finally, in 1917, Pope Benedict XV promulgated the first comprehensive *Code of Canon Law*, consisting of 2414 canons.

The Second Vatican Council (1962–1965) addressed many topics that would have a major impact on the current formulation of canon law. Pope John XXIII had first called for a revision of canon law in 1959, but it was not until 1967 that work was begun under Paul VI. In 1983, John Paul II finally promulgated the new version of canon law, emphasizing the need to interpret it in light of Vatican II.

The new version of the Code has 1752 canons. Its seven "books" concern "General Norms"; "The People of God"; "The Teaching Office of the Church"; "The Office of Sanctifying in the Church"; "The Temporal Goods of the Church"; "Sanctions in the Church"; and "Processes." Most canonical issues involve canons from several books of the Code; this is certainly true of excommunication cases.

4. OK, so what does the word "excommunication" literally mean?

In this context, *excommunication* literally means "out of full communion" with the Catholic Church. Because excommunication can be imposed only on a Catholic (that is, one who is in full communion with the Church according to canon 205), excommunication deprives one of the fullness of the communion that he or she previously enjoyed.

It is sometimes said that the Church never excommunicates anyone; rather, people excommunicate themselves. There is some truth to this saying if it is understood to mean that excommunication is only incurred as the result of an individual's actions. It is misleading, however, if it is meant to suggest that the Church lacks the power or authority to render such decisions, or that individual members of the Church can make up their own conditions for being in full communion.

Excommunication does not mean that one is no longer a Christian (because Christian baptism imprints an indelible character on the soul) or no longer a Catholic (for although there *are* ways to renounce one's Catholic identity, excommunication is not one of them). It does mean, though, that one is deprived of the benefits of full communion with the Catholic Church.

5. What does it mean to be "in full communion" with the Church?

Canonically speaking, to be in full communion with the Church means sharing in its beliefs, participating in its sacramental life, and complying with its governing authority (canon 205). At an even deeper level, full communion means all these things, but also (as the Second Vatican Council teaches) sharing in the "spirit of Christ" (*Lumen Gentium*, 14). Catholics who are in full communion with the Church are striving to live according to the teachings of Christ and to follow His will in all things.

6. Can Protestants be excommunicated? What about Jews or Muslims?

No. As we have said, only Catholics in full communion with the Church can be excommunicated.

First, non-Christians—Jews and Muslims, for example—are not subject to ecclesiastical law. They are, of course, bound by natural law and by the laws of their own traditions and countries, but they are not subject to the laws or penalties of the Catholic Church. While the Church can and does pray for and dialogue with these groups, it does not legislate for them.

As a practical matter, the same is basically true of Protestants and other separated Christians, but their situation is slightly different. As baptized Christians, these groups are closer to the Catholic Church and are more clearly called to respect the laws Christ has revealed for His followers—laws which are contained in their fullness within the Catholic Church. But while the Church carries on exchanges and cooperative efforts with separated Christians, and while she considers them more closely bound to the behavior expected of all Christians, for historical and practical reasons non-Catholic Christians are not subject to canon law. Thus, they are not subject to ecclesiastical penalties such as excommunication.

7. In the previous answer, you mentioned "natural law." What is this?

The natural law is a set of principles for right living that is based not on religious tenets or doctrinal positions, but rather on the very fact that we are all human beings. While Catholic thinkers are among the most articulate defenders of natural law, it is not a Catholic—or even Christian—creation. In many places, civil law and canon law both uphold principles that, in reality, are founded on natural law. Maybe an example would help.

After World War II, many Nazis tried to escape punishment for their genocidal crimes by claiming that the persecution of Jews was legal under German law. Allied prosecutors countered—correctly—that any civil law that tries to legalize the persecution of innocent beings is, in fact, no law at all. They made this argument, not on the basis of American or British law, or even on religious law, but on the basis of natural law.

The exact content of natural law is the subject of much study and debate. Natural law does not delve deeply into minutiae; its broadest outlines are clear and bind all human persons, regardless of nationality or religious affiliation. For example, natural law requires us to keep the promises we make, even if those promises are not technically recognized as contracts. Or again, natural law requires us to avoid committing abortion and euthanasia, even if the state legalizes such practices.

Christians are, of course, bound to honor the natural law, but Christ has given His followers additional precepts to follow. He expects Christians to go beyond the just requirements of natural law and to make the law of love a central part of their life.

8. **Are people still being excommunicated, or is excommunication a relic of the "pre-Vatican II" Church?**

The Church's canon law on excommunication is still in force, and it has been (with some reforms) continuously since the conclusion of the Second Vatican Council in 1965. (The Second Vatican Council—commonly called Vatican II—was the 21st *ecumenical* council in Church history, in which more than 2,000 bishops from around the world met and enacted many important reforms.)

Unfortunately, grave sin still exists, and some grave sins are also canonical crimes that can result in excommunication. Admittedly, there have been fewer cases of excommunication since Vatican II, but this is perhaps more a result of the Church having its attention focused on other matters than those raised in most excommunication cases. Moreover, major changes in the penal procedural law went into effect with the 1983 Code. These technical changes took a long time to study and appreciate, and in the years following the release of the revised code, many ecclesiastical leaders simply did not want to try excommunication cases until the new procedures were better understood.

As the dust from the Second Vatican Council continues to settle, and as clearer outlines of what is and what is not sound Catholic thought and behavior continues to emerge, look for the consequences (including excommunication) of violating Church teaching to occur more frequently.

9.   Is excommunication really necessary?

In the same way that punishment is sometimes necessary in other social or political settings—for example, a child who loses dessert for not eating his peas or an arsonist who goes to jail for insurance fraud—so excommunication is sometimes necessary in a religious setting.

Punishment serves important functions: it teaches individuals in clear ways that certain behavior is wrong, and it upholds the principles upon which small and large societies live together in peace. In the society known as the Catholic Church, certain behaviors are so serious and so disruptive that they warrant the imposition of the most severe penalty the Church has—excommunication.

Obviously, punishment of the innocent is a grave injustice, as is punishment that does not fit the crime. Every effort must be made to ensure that these injustices do not occur. But punishment that responds in a measured way to the offense, and that is imposed only after hearing the evidence and allowing the right of defense, can actually serve many ends.

10. How has excommunication been used in the history of the Church?

In basically the same manner it is used today: as a way of declaring the gravity of certain behaviors and to inflict justly deserved consequences on those committing such actions. Over the centuries, the Church has always been concerned that excommunication might be used too frequently or for offenses that (today at least) seem less serious. In fact, since the late 19th century, the unmistakable trend has been to reduce the number of offenses that can be punished by excommunication.

The Church understands that, depending on the situation, an excommunication might have some impact in areas of life outside of religion or theology. For example, to excommunicate a king for starting an unjust war might have an impact on how that war turns out. While not blind to such considerations, the Church's primary focus is always on an individual's welfare, on helping him to accept responsibility for his actions and repent of wrongdoing. It is important to realize that excommunication (or, indeed, any ecclesiastical consequence to behavior) is not imposed by the Church on purely public relations grounds.

11. Are there other kinds of Church penalties besides excommunication? If so, what are they?

While excommunication is the Church's severest sanction, it is not the only penalty she can impose. Over the centuries, the Church has developed a fairly straightforward system of sanctions with which it can regulate ecclesiastical discipline.

All sanctions in the Church fall into one of two classes: *censures*, specifically excommunication, interdict, and suspension; and *expiatory penalties*, such as loss of office or rank, orders to reside in certain locales (or outside them, for that matter), and still others. Dismissal from the clerical state—basically the perpetual expulsion from ordained ministry—is the most severe expiatory penalty.

These two classes of penalties serve very different purposes in the Church. Censures are designed to bring about personal reform in the offender. If there are any reasonable alternatives to imposing a censure in order to achieve such personal reform, then those alternatives must be tried before a censure can be used. Moreover, once a censure—even excommunication— achieves its desired result, it must promptly cease. The popular impression of excommunication as a sort of spiritual "life-in-prison" is quite wrong. The only people who are excommunicated "for life" are those who choose to be.

Expiatory penalties, on the other hand, are imposed as a way of upholding good order and of vindicating the norms of justice in the Church. Expiatory penalties— such as deprivation of office, written apologies, even community service—are tailored to fit the offense and, if imposed, are generally enforceable regardless of the disposition of the offender. Naturally, one hopes that a personal change of heart accompanies the performance of the penalty, but once the penalty is satisfied, it ceases, even if the offender has not learned the error of his ways.

12. How is a person excommunicated? What is the process?

There are basically two ways one can be excommunicated. Assuming that one has committed a gravely sinful action that is subject to excommunication, one might either be "automatically" excommunicated or excommunicated in a formal process. Let's first consider "automatic" excommunication.

The number of offenses for which "automatic" excommunication is the punishment dropped steadily during the past century, and it dropped dramatically when the current *Code of Canon Law* went into effect in 1983. We will talk more about those specifics later, but several points need to be remembered whenever we're talking about "automatic" (technically known as *latae sententiae*) excommunications.

For starters, "automatic" penalties are more difficult to incur than it would seem given their "automatic" nature. A number of canons work together to restrict the scope of "automatic" sanctions in the Church (e.g., cc. 18, 1321– 1324). Moreover, even if an automatic excommunication is incurred, its external or visible consequences are diminished as compared to excommunication incurred after a formal process (c. 1331). Finally, Eastern Catholic canon law no longer contains any automatic penalties, and there is even some question as to how long their automatic character will be retained in Western canon law. For all that, "automatic" penalties are still on the books, and they deserve respect.

The other way that excommunication can be imposed is by a formal process (known technically as *ferendae sententiae*, c. 1314). This formal process is either "administrative" or "judicial" (c. 1341). Both methods include such personal safeguards as notice of charges, protection of the right to be heard, and various rights of appeal. Indeed, modern canon law seems strongly to prefer judicial trials for excommunication (c. 1425), but some high-profile excommunication cases have recently been heard *administratively* by Roman congregations operating with papal approval. (For example, Archbishop Marcel Lefebvre was excommunicated administratively after he consecrated bishops without papal approval.)

Whether it be administratively or judicially, the infliction of excommunication through a formal process carries some higher implications for enforcement than is usual for so-called "automatic" excommunication (c. 1331). This is probably a result of the fact that formal processes help make sure every mitigating circumstance has been weighed in the defendant's favor and that a conviction in a formal process is based on more deliberate findings of serious offenses.

Remember—the Church is like a loving mother who does not want to discipline her children too harshly. Rather, she only wants to use the amount of punishment necessary to correct and train her children in the right path—that is, according to the truth.

13. What are some of the things people can be excommunicated for?

Today's list of excommunicable offenses is much shorter than it was at other times in Church history. There has been a conscious effort by ecclesiastical authority—especially since the late 19th century and even more so after Vatican II—to reduce the number of offenses for which excommunication can be used. The Catholic Church is clearly restricting her most serious punishment to the most serious offenses. Why? Because, as stated earlier, the Church wishes to use censures only to the degree necessary for repentance.

Under current canon law, only certain crimes are directly punishable by excommunication. They are: apostasy, heresy, or schism (c. 1364); desecration of the Eucharist (c. 1367); physical attack on the pope (c. 1370); absolution of an accomplice (c. 1378); simulated celebration of Mass or confession (c. 1378); unauthorized consecration of bishops (c. 1382); violation of the sacramental seal by the confessor or by others (c. 1388); and procuring abortion (c. 1398). One can easily see that these types of offenses are those that could cause great disturbance in the Church.

Strictly speaking, there are other offenses that might result in an excommunication, but these are quite rare. For example, the special pontifical law on papal conclaves (i.e., the special assembly of cardinals in which a new pope is elected) imposes an excommunication on one who violates the secrecy of a conclave—obviously, that is not something many of us *could* do, even if we wanted to! More practically, under certain circumstances, one's offensive conduct could exacerbate behavior that, in itself, was not subject to excommunication, but, due to circumstances, makes excommunication a possibility. We will discuss this more in a later question, but for now, the main point is that excommunication is limited to only a few, very serious and well-defined offenses.

14. I had heard that Catholics who divorce and then remarry outside the Church are excommunicated. Is this true?

In the United States, this was true for nearly a hundred years, but it is not true today. In 1884, the Third Plenary Council of Baltimore received permission from the Holy See to impose an "automatic" excommunication on American Catholics who divorced and, without petitioning for and receiving a *declaration of nullity* (commonly called an *annulment*), remarried in a civil or other non-Catholic ceremony. This special penal law, applicable only in America, remained in effect until 1977 when the American bishops asked for and received Rome's permission to drop the penalty of excommunication in these cases. Since then, American Catholics who divorce and remarry outside the Church are not excommunicated (though, in most cases, the Church does not recognize the validity of those weddings).

Moreover, by operation of what later became canon 1313 of the 1983 Code, those who were already excommunicated at the time saw their penalty lifted, even though they lacked the change of heart that normally must precede the lifting of a censure such as excommunication.

It is important to understand that lifting the penalty of excommunication did not mean that the Church suddenly recognized these marriages as being valid, or that marrying outside the Church was no longer seen as gravely wrong and spiritually harmful. Persons who are divorced and remarried outside the Church even today are generally prohibited (under c. 915) from receiving the Eucharist until they rectify their situation in accord with canon law. The Congregation for the Doctrine of the Faith reiterated this point as recently as 1994 in its *Letter on the Reception of the Eucharist by Divorced and Remarried Catholics.*

By the way, the phrase "outside the Church" does not mean "outside of a church building," but rather marrying in disregard of the Church's authority to regulate the marriages of her members. Some people are confused on this point.

15. This sounds like the Church can change moral laws? Is this right?

No. The fundamental moral laws given to us by Christ—and, for that matter, the natural laws grounded in human nature—are not subject to change by any authority, even the Church. But we need to be careful here.

Our *knowledge* of the moral law can change over time, resulting in what some might mistake as a change in the moral law itself. Also, the *consequences* for violating moral laws might change over time to fit changed circumstances, again resulting in what some might mistake as changes in the moral law. Moreover, many laws in the Church and the state might *seem* to be enactments of moral law, but in reality are not—meaning that changes in them are not changes in the moral law in the first place.

16. Are there different "types" of excommunication?

Not really. There are two *ways* that one might incur excommunication—namely, "automatically" or by a formal process—but this difference relates only to the *manner* by which one is excommunicated, not the type of penalty that is incurred. So-called "automatic" or *ipso facto* penalties carry fewer visible consequences than do formal penalties (see c. 1331), but this does not result in there being two types of excommunication, just different degrees of application.

Historically, there were different types of excommunication. They were sometimes called "major" excommunication (basically, what we know today as excommunication) or "minor" excommunication (or what we would today call *interdict*). And, even into the 20th century, there were categories of excommunicants (*vitandi* and *tolerati*, see question 29), but today, this distinction is gone as well. Finally, the term *anathema* was sometimes used to describe a more formal liturgical imposition or declaration of excommunication, but this too is gone. Today, one is either excommunicated or not excommunicated.

17. Isn't excommunication an offense against charity? Doesn't Jesus preach love and forgiveness?

It is true that Jesus preaches love and forgiveness, as does His Church. There is nothing the Church wants more for someone laboring under an excommunication (or any other censure) than to seek forgiveness and be reconciled with the Mystical Body of Christ. That is one of the reasons, in fact, that the Church classifies excommunication as a *censure*, because censures are subject to prompt cessation upon an individual's change of heart and personal resolve not to commit the action again (cc. 1312, 1358).

You see, unlike an *expiatory penalty* (cc. 1312, 1336) that is imposed regardless of the sorrow of the offender for his actions (one might think of having to pay a traffic fine even if you're really sorry you ran that red light), censures—even grave censures such as excommunication—can be enforced only until the offender repents of his actions. Once that conversion of heart is manifested, however, canon law itself (to say nothing of the example of Jesus) requires that those excommunicated be promptly and formally reconciled with the Church.

18. Who has the power to excommunicate?

The pope has the power to excommunicate (c. 331), as do those relatively few Vatican officials who act in his name for certain types of cases (c. 360). Likewise, diocesan bishops (c. 381) can impose excommunication, and, in certain types of cases, Roman and diocesan judicial tribunals can pass sentences of excommunication after a trial (cc. 1401, 1405, and 1425). Ecumenical councils have this power as well, though it has not been exercised for many centuries (c. 337).

19. How can an excommunicated person be reconciled with the Church?

The reconciliation of an excommunicated person depends on various factors, including *what* one was excommunicated for, *how* one was excommunicated, and what the *circumstances* of the reconciliation would be.

If the penalty of excommunication was formally imposed or declared, then as a general rule only the same authority that imposed or declared the penalty can lift it. In this regard, canon law is much like civil law in providing for an orderly manner of lifting penalties duly imposed. Strictly speaking, there are some other ecclesiastical officials who can remit a formal penalty such as excommunication, but that discussion turns on technical points and, in any case, is so rare that we need not worry about it here. (If you're really curious about it though, check out cc. 1354-1356).

Because excommunication, like all censures, is designed chiefly to bring about personal reform in the offender, canon law contains yet another way of being reconciled with the Church. This method is available especially if the excommunication was an "automatic" one, but in some ways it can be applied even in the face of formally imposed or declared excommunications. That way is sacramental confession (c. 1357). Confessors are authorized to lift certain kinds of censures, including excommunication, in confession, provided the penitent agrees to present quickly a proper request for remission of penalty to the competent authority, and of course, provided he or she has expressed sorrow for the action itself. It is yet another way that the Church offers her members to achieve reconciliation as quickly as possible, without losing sight of the seriousness of the actions that caused the rupture in the first place.

Finally, in all these considerations, one must keep in mind that certain excommunications constitute what are technically known as "reserved offenses"—that is, ecclesiastical crimes whose investigation, eventual application, and possible remission, are reserved to higher Church authority, usually the Apostolic See (i.e., the pope). Examples of this would be desecration of the Eucharist (c. 1367), assault on the Roman Pontiff (c. 1370), or consecration of a bishop without papal mandate (c. 1382). In these cases, Rome must be approached for remission of any excommunication that might have been incurred. By the way, the number of "reserved cases" has also been reduced in recent decades, making it easier for people who might fall under excommunication to find reconciliation.

If this all strikes you as a bit complicated, you're right. All the more reason, though, to avoid those things than can result in such a severe penalty.

20. Is the Catholic Church the only religious organization that excommunicates its members?

Since this question turns on issues that are more historical than canonical, I've asked Catholic researcher Brian Simboli, Ph.D., to offer his thoughts.

In the Protestant Reformation, the Catholic practices of penance and absolution were not retained, but those Protestant churches that regarded the congregation as having the power to hand down penalties on their members continued to impose excommunication. A modern day U.S. example of this exists in the Congregationalist churches.

In post-1945 Germany, certain churches stipulated that pastors and congregational leaders could bar individuals from taking communion. A Church of England canon provides for excommunication. The Amish practice of "shunning" involves almost complete avoidance of an individual for limited or permanent periods, depending on the offense, and can be ended if the shunned person repents. Excommunication is also part of the Mormon faith.

In Judaic tradition, there were four types of excommunication, the strictest of which involved not being allowed to hear or teach the Torah and shunning by persons other than the excommunicants' immediate family. In the modern period, this type of excommunication is practiced in Israel by the very orthodox community.

In Buddhist monasticism, individuals can be let go from their monastic order if they engage in certain types of wrongdoing.

Nonetheless, while these other religious groups may use the term "excommunication" when "kicking out" members who go astray or are otherwise deemed undesirable, the Catholic practice of excommunication is unique. None of these other religions possesses the apostolic authority given the Catholic Church by Christ Himself. Nor do they possess a developed legal and canonical tradition akin to that of the Church, whose guiding principle has always been to codify its laws in a way that protects the rights of all its members.

21. Is there any support in the Bible for excommunication?

Yes. In various ways, the Bible clearly supports the concept of excommunication. The passages mentioned below convey the sense that while individuals can be excluded from the community, this exclusion should be seen as a means to reforming them and bringing them back to full communion.

Matthew 18:15-18 speaks of correcting a brother or sister in Christ who has done wrong. At first, one is to confront the person; if this does not work, one or two other people should assist in the confronting. Finally, if even this does not work, the community intervenes, at which point one must treat the individual in the same way pagans or tax collectors would be treated. (The reference in Matthew 18:18 to binding and loosing has been understood as a reference to the Church's authority with respect to doctrine and discipline, of which the power to excommunicate is only one example.) 1 Corinthians 5:2, 13 suggest the need to expel an individual who has engaged in sexual immorality from the community.

These strong statements are counterbalanced by other passages. The parable of Matthew 13:28-30 suggests that some evil persons are not to be "weeded out" while they are on earth, lest good persons be "weeded out" with them. In 2 Corinthians 2:5-1, Paul emphasizes the need to forgive a wrongdoer who has undergone sufficient punishment, while 1 Corinthians 5:4-5 strongly condemns a sinner, but leaves open the possibility of his salvation.

22. By what authority does the Church excommunicate someone?

Quite simply, by the authority given it by Christ Himself (see Matthew 16).

From a purely sociological point of view, one could say that an organization has the right to determine rules for its own membership and, within the limits of its authority, can impose consequences on members who violate those rules. While this might be an interesting point to raise, in reality, the Church's authority in this matter is not a human convention, but rather a God-given responsibility.

We need to remember that when God chose to reveal Himself to mankind, He didn't just drop a book out of the sky. Rather, he established a community to which He revealed Himself and gave the authority to teach in His name. In the Old Testament, the Lord gave the Law through Moses and, later, gave authority to the priests to lead the people in worship and sacrifice. In the New Testament, Jesus endowed the twelve apostles with divine authority to sanctify, teach, and govern in His name. This authority, in turn, was passed on to their successors, the bishops, and in a special way to the successor of Peter, the head of the apostles—the pope.

The Church serves as the teacher and interpreter of God's revelation as contained in Sacred Scripture and Tradition. While not divinely revealed, canon law draws on the authority of the Church.

23. Is an excommunicated person condemned to hell?

God Himself judges the state of each person's soul immediately after death, and His perfect judgment decides the individual's fate—whether to indescribable sufferings in hell forever, purgatory for a time, or directly to unimaginable happiness in heaven for eternity. The Church does not pretend to judge the state of anyone's soul. At the same time, however, we know that God established His Church on earth and entrusted it with great authority. One who dies in a state of excommunication (or "unreconciled," as the traditional phrase puts it), goes before God with the decision of His Church that he was not in full communion with it (a state that can only arise as a result of certain grave sins), and that one's relationship with the Church was not repaired prior to death.

24. What are the practical effects of excommunication?

As outlined in canon 1331, they are chiefly as follows:

Prohibition against *ministerial* participation (e.g., a priest celebrating Mass, a layperson serving as a lector or extraordinary minister of the Eucharist) in the sacrifice of the Eucharist or ceremonies of worship (e.g., Mass and the Liturgy of the Hours); prohibition against celebrating the sacraments (e.g., performing weddings, baptisms, etc.) or celebrating sacramentals (e.g., giving blessings), or receiving the sacraments (e.g., getting married, being confirmed, being ordained); and exercising ecclesiastical office or authority. Note that nothing in the list prohibits one from attending Mass, reciting the Liturgy of the Hours, or from receiving blessings. Indeed, those bound to Mass attendance (as are all Catholics) or to praying the Liturgy of the Hours (as are clergy and religious) must still honor these obligations.

If a person has been *formally* excommunicated, the situation gets somewhat more complicated. Depending on circumstances, such a person who attempts to take a ministerial role in Mass is to be prevented from doing so, or at least the liturgical action should cease. If the person holds ecclesiastical office, then any actions taken in that office are basically null and of no legal effect. Such persons cannot obtain other ecclesiastical offices and might even forfeit the Church's financial support if they hold a paid position.

We should keep in mind that many of these consequences also fall on those who, while not excommunicated, are *interdicted* under canon 1332, and some of them even affect those who are *suspended* under canon 1333. In brief, just because one is not excommunicated does not necessarily mean that one is not subject to some other form of canonical penalty for seriously disruptive actions.

25. What are the spiritual effects of excommunication on one's soul?

When a person is under excommunication, he is deprived of the benefits of full communion with the Catholic Church. Those things include the right to participate in its sacramental life and to exercise various ecclesiastical offices.

26. What are the possible physical consequences of excommunication? Is one subject to demonic afflictions, injury, even death?

Excommunication is a spiritual penalty, so I can't imagine what *physical* consequences would flow from it. None are envisioned in canon law. As for the devil, certainly he prowls about the world seeking the destruction of souls, and he works more effectively on those who are in grave sin (such as would be, objectively speaking, those under the penalty of excommunication). But, in itself, excommunication does not place one at the mercy of Satan, nor cast one beyond the reach of God's saving grace. Still, one would want to be reconciled with His Church on earth as quickly as possible, lest one tempt fate.

27. Can an excommunicated person enter a church?

Yes. In fact, they are obligated to do so once a week! It's called Sunday Mass, an obligation to which persons under excommunication are still bound. Those formally excommunicated are prohibited from receiving the Eucharist and from having any "ministerial participation" in Mass (e.g., serving as a lector or Eucharistic minister), but not from *attending* Mass (c. 1331).

In early Church history, there was a time when those who had fallen into grave sin (including some sins which today could result in excommunication) *were* prohibited from entering a church. These penitents were, as part of their reconciliation, required to remain outside the church during the liturgy and to ask for the prayers of those entering the church for worship. At a later stage of their reconciliation, penitents were allowed to stand in the back of the church, and only upon full reconciliation could they later rejoin the congregation. This process illustrated how far one's sins could remove him or her from the Mystical Body of Christ, and it symbolized reconciliation with His Church in a graphic way. In any case, while the Church could, if it wanted, prohibit excommunicants or other offenders from entering its places of worship, this is not the present law.

28. Are Catholics required to "shun" someone who has been excommunicated, similar to the practice of strict Protestant sects such as the Mennonites and Amish?

No. At various times in Church history, there was sometimes an obligation to avoid certain excommunicants. In fact, for a while, excommunicants were divided into two groups—*tolerandi* and *vitandi*—that is, ones that could be tolerated and others that had to be avoided. This distinction was still found in canon law as late as the early 20th century, but it has been dropped from current law as being unworkable given the way modern societies are set up. We can and should pray for the reconciliation of those laboring under an excommunication (or other ecclesiastical censure) since canon law makes very clear that reconciliation with the Church is available at any time they choose to be reconciled.

29. How can I find out that someone has been excommunicated? Is there a published list?

There is no master list of excommunicated persons. Sometimes, though, in cases of importance to a large number of people, public notice of the excommunication is issued. A good example of this is the case of Archbishop Marcel Lefebvre, who ordained four bishops without the pope's approval in 1988. Such cases—and they are few in number—are usually reported in the official journal of the Holy See, *Acta Apostolicae Sedis*. You are not likely to subscribe to this publication, but it can usually be found in Catholic college and seminary libraries. It's a difficult journal to read, and I would suggest asking for help before plowing through it. Another place to look would be in the Vatican newspaper *L'Osservatore Romano* (which publishes a weekly English edition), but again, if an excommunication notice appears there, it has probably received considerable publicity elsewhere.

Excommunications that occur at the diocesan level can be reported in diocesan newspapers or on websites, but strictly speaking, there is no requirement that bishops or tribunals make these decisions public. Neither, however, is there a prohibition against their doing so, and some of the important purposes served by excommunication (such as public reaffirmation of how wrong certain kinds of behavior are) are lost if notice of the excommunication is withheld from the public. Finally, persons who have been excommunicated are free to tell whomever they wish.

30. If I am convicted of a crime in civil court, I have the right to appeal the verdict. Is there any similar process of appeal in the Church for someone who has been excommunicated?

Yes. In fact, those convicted under canon law enjoy some procedural rights not extended to those convicted under civil law. A basic right of appeal (and this applies regardless of whether the excommunication was imposed administratively or judicially) runs all the way up the procedural ladder ultimately to the pope himself. Thus, a person excommunicated by one level of ecclesiastical authority can still appeal to a higher level automatically.

Importantly, though—and in sharp contrast to most civil law procedures—if one appeals a canonical conviction, the actual imposition of the penalty must be suspended during the appeal process (cc. 1353, 1723). This is another example of how slow the Church is to impose any penalty, especially grave penalties such as excommunication.

For that matter, a variety of rights are recognized for those facing any kind of ecclesiastical prosecution, including the right to be heard by an authorized and unbiased tribunal (cc. 221, 1412, 1421, 1448, 1501), the right to represent one's self or to be represented by canonical counsel (cc. 1477, 1481, 1723), the right to be heard and to submit evidence (numerous canons, including cc. 1527, 1725), the right to call witnesses (c. 1547), the right to a public statement of exoneration if warranted (c. 1727), and so on.

Canon law, while operating differently in some ways from the legal procedures that we are accustomed to in "common law" nations, is a much older and time-tested legal system that has historically served as a model of fairness for other legal systems. While every legal system has its faults and can make mistakes, canon law is scrupulous about defending the rights of the accused.

31. If one is excommunicated by his local bishop, does this excommunication apply to just his diocese or throughout the Church?

Excommunication applies everywhere in the Church. We need to remember that the Church is the Mystical

Body of Christ—every baptized Catholic is linked to this body, much like your hand is linked to your arm and to the rest of your body. This is why excommunication, even if imposed by a local bishop, applies throughout the entire Church.

32. What role has excommunication played in Church history?

As an historical question, let's turn again to Catholic researcher Brian Simboli, Ph.D., for his insights on this issue.

Excommunication has played a significant role at important junctures in Church history (though some of the examples cited below would be considered problematic from the view of the current *Code of Canon Law*). Excommunication has also figured in struggles between church and state—for example, in the eleventh-century struggle between Pope Gregory VII and King Henry IV and in the events surrounding Thomas à Becket's murder in 1170. In the Reformation, excommunications were used to counter the emergence of Protestantism. After defying the orders of a Church council, Martin Luther rejected the authority of the papacy and was excommunicated in 1521. King Henry VIII of England, after rejecting the papacy and establishing himself as the head of the Church of England, was excommunicated and his subjects freed from their allegiance to him in 1538.

Excommunication has also played a role in modern struggles. New Orleans Archbishop Joseph Rummel in 1962 excommunicated the racist segregationist Leander Perez, who repented before his death in 1969. In 1975,

Bishop Aparicio of El Salvador excommunicated government officials for torturing a priest. Excommunication has been used in the civil rights struggle against abortionists and pro-choice policies. A Planned Parenthood director was excommunicated in 1986 and resigned. In 1990, Bishop Rene Gracida of Corpus Christi, Texas excommunicated two abortionists. Much present discussion centers on what penalties, including excommunication, are appropriate for the many politicians who hypocritically describe themselves as Catholic but who support pro-choice laws and policies.

33. Can the pope be excommunicated?

Certainly we know that popes can make mistakes and render poor decisions, and history shows that popes can sin, sometimes gravely. The charism of papal *infallibility* (i.e., the divinely-given protection from doctrinal error when making solemn pronouncements on matters of faith and morality) must never be confused with papal *impeccability* (i.e., freedom from sin). So, popes could commit actions that are mortally sinful, and if they die in that state, they would face the same judgment as any of us.

Upon examining the grounds for excommunication, two of them—physically attacking the pope and performing unauthorized episcopal ordinations (cc. 1370, 1382)—seem impossible for a pope to commit, but all the others are at least theoretically possible. If pressed on the matter, though, most canon lawyers would say that popes cannot be formally excommunicated, for the simple reason that no authority on earth (not even the college of bishops gathered in an ecumenical council; see c. 336) is allowed to issue official judgments on him (c. 1404). If, God forbid, such a case should ever arise, the solution would not be found in canon law, but in the divine assurance by Christ that He would never abandon His Church.

34. Could a Church official be excommunicated if his or her primary motive for continued Church service becomes personal gain or achieving a higher Church position?

Working for the Church, whether in ordained ministry or in various apostolates, is about service, not power. Even the power that comes with certain ecclesiastical offices is given to serve others. Those who enter Church service out of selfish motives (and history offers some examples here) do a disservice to the mission of Christ and His Church.

Except for cases of clear abuse of office, though, it would be difficult canonically to prosecute cases in which one's motives for personal gain actually constituted a crime. A moral failing, perhaps, but not a crime in itself, canonically speaking.

35. How many people are formally excommunicated by the Church each year?

There is no set figure and no quota. The Church would like to see no one excommunicated in any year. By any measure, though, publicly-incurred excommunications are rare events.

36. What does the *Catechism of the Catholic Church* say about excommunication?

The *Catechism* says that excommunication is applicable for especially grave sins and "impedes the reception of the sacraments and the exercise of certain ecclesiastical acts" (CCC 1463), such as exercising an ecclesiastical office.

So while the *Catechism* talks about how serious excommunication is and notes that the Church requires special steps for lifting it, these provisions are relaxed when the excommunicant is on the verge of death. Notice that the *Catechism* section on excommunication appears in a chapter entitled "The Sacraments of Healing" (chapter two), in an article about the sacrament of Penance. The discussion of excommunication (CCC 1463) immediately follows a section that starts out by speaking of forgiveness of sins. Excommunication thus fits in with the spirit of the sacrament of confession, whose goal is to restore friendship with God (see CCC 1468).

37. Can someone be excommunicated if he or she leaves the faith or joins another Catholic rite (e.g., Melkite, Byzantine, etc.)?

No. All Catholics, whether of Western or Eastern-rite, have the option under certain circumstances to change rites (or what are known more technically as Churches *sui iuris*, "of their own law") since all of these Churches are in full communion with Rome (c. 112).

But maybe you are thinking not of Catholic Eastern-rite Churches, but rather of Orthodox Churches. This is a different situation. The various Orthodox Churches are not in full communion with Rome. So for a Catholic to join one of them is, objectively speaking, an act of schism. Such an action could put one at risk of excommunication under canon 1364, which also punishes apostasy and heresy. The recent trend in the Church, however, has been to react to defections from the faith that involve Orthodox churches without formally imposing canonical sanctions.

38. What if a Catholic who is immature or truly ignorant joins another Christian denomination, but on being instructed returns to the Church? Would they still incur excommunication?

Factors such as "immaturity" and being "truly ignorant" militate against incurring the *moral* guilt of mortal sin in the first place, and without at least that degree of responsibility, one cannot be excommunicated. In addition, these same kinds of factors also impact on the *legal* requirements that must be proven to impose the penalty of excommunication (cc. 1321–1324). The individual you describe might be acting wrongly, and might even face some level of responsibility for his deeds, but it is unlikely such a person has incurred excommunication.

39. Can a doctor who performs euthanasia be excommunicated?

One can only be excommunicated for committing a canonical crime for which excommunication is an authorized punishment. Under the current Code, euthanasia is not a crime for which excommunication can be imposed, but that being said, three important points must be mentioned.

First, from a moral point of view, euthanasia is a form of murder and, as such, is already punishable under canon 1397 (which does not itself authorize excommunication). Nevertheless, if one who is punished for euthanasia under canon 1397 in turn ignores that penalty (or, as we might say in civil law, shows "contempt of court"), the penalty can be escalated under canon 1393. This canon is much more open-ended about what sanctions could be imposed. Most canonists would agree that, under certain circumstances, excommunication could be a "just penalty" under such a canon, and one who practices euthanasia could aggravate his situation to the point where he might face excommunication.

Second, canon 1399 allows ecclesiastical leaders to punish any violation of divine or canon law (and euthanasia is prohibited under both) if there is an urgent need to address the situation. It is not difficult to imagine circumstances in which this would be applicable. Again, the penalty for cases heard under this canon is open-ended, and could include excommunication.

Third, the Church—at the level of the Holy See or at the local diocesan level—has the authority at any time to enact direct penal canons on actions that are seriously immoral in themselves and that disturb the good order of society. Over the centuries, the Church's list of crimes has changed in response to the needs of time and place. If the Church, faced with the rising specter of euthanasia, decided to punish that offense with the penalty of excommunication, it would be acting completely within its authority.

40. If a deacon or lay person tries to absolve a penitent or attempts to perform the sacred acts proper to a priest (e.g., celebrate Mass, anoint the sick, etc.), does this warrant excommunication?

All of these examples fall squarely under the terms of canons 1378–1379, but the penalty for such actions is not excommunication, but rather *interdict* or *suspension*. At the same time, though, these canons admit the possibility that excommunication might be appropriate under certain circumstances. This conclusion is supported by canon 1326, which allows ecclesiastical officials to increase penalties when the offense was committed by someone abusing their ecclesiastical rank or privileges. People have a right to know that those acting in sacred capacities have the power and authority to do so. The Church takes prompt action in response to the pretended celebration of the sacraments.

41. If someone publicly desecrates the Holy Eucharist or makes a mockery of any sacrament of the Church, is this grounds for excommunication?

Desecration of the Eucharist is a grave sin, and it is punishable by excommunication under canon 1367. There is no requirement that the desecration be "public," as one might commonly understand that term, but just provable. Indeed, this offense is so serious that excommunication is "reserved" to the Apostolic See, a matter we discuss in question 19. Finally, I would note that that if a bishop, priest, or deacon, commits this act, he may also be expelled from the clerical state.

42. What if a Catholic, whether in his or her personal relations or publicly as a member of the media, consistently and deliberately denigrates or twists the official teachings of the Church?

The Church certainly recognizes the awesome power and great potential for good that modern means of communication offer. In 1963, the Second Vatican Council issued an entire document on social communications, *Inter mirifica*, and many subsequent ecclesiastical statements have followed up on this conciliar declaration. Several provisions in the 1983 *Code of Canon Law* relate to social communications, and they are basically designed to help Catholics understand that modern communications are tools that need to be used responsibly.

In particular, however, canon 1369 focuses on people who abuse the means of communications to spread contempt for the Church or of good morals, and authorizes the imposition of a "just penalty" on them. Obviously, the broad phrase "just penalty" can mean any sanction already contained in the *Code of Canon Law*, or penalties more directly suited to remedy the offense being committed. Examples might be retractions of utterances, public penances, or the performance of works of mercy designed to set an example of good where once there was harm.

Most canon lawyers would agree that, under the right circumstances, a "just penalty" for such an offense could be excommunication, but they would probably hold that lesser sanctions must be tried first. In particular, the question of excommunicating Catholic politicians for pro-abortion support has been studied extensively. Most canonists agree that, as the law reads now, such pro-abortion activities—because they only lend support to abortion but do not themselves result in an abortion—are not directly subject to excommunication under the abortion canon (c. 1398). Recently, more attention has been focused on the harm such men and women are causing as a result of their use of the means of social communication to spread disrespect for pre-born babies. Thus, attention is being given to taking penal action against them under canon 1369.

43. What can be done about anti-life Catholic politicians who contribute to the spread of abortion in our society? Do Church leaders have to stand by and watch these people pursue their evil goals in the halls of government?

There are a number of ways pro-abortion Catholic politicians might face canonical sanctions for their pro-abortion activities. I mentioned one previously—namely, canon 1369, which authorizes a "just penalty" for those who use speeches, writings, and other forms of social communication to gravely injure good morals. It is quite possible that some of the more militant pro-abortion politicians fall under the terms of this canon. Other canons might apply to the situations as well, depending on the facts.

Moreover, the Church itself might decide to enact special legislation in this area, knowing that public advocacy of abortion is creating a climate in which people feel it is acceptable to kill pre-born babies.

Besides looking at sanction canons, increasing attention is being given to using canon 915 in the sacramental realm as a way to counteract a politician's actions in supporting abortion. Such activity is gravely sinful in itself and where it can be shown that the politician's pro-abortion advocacy is both manifest and obstinate, canon 915 might result in the eventual denial of the Eucharist.

What it boils down to is this: Conscientious pro-lifers should not let themselves think that canon 1398 is sufficient to convict pro-abortion Catholic politicians if only it were tried, but neither should they be discouraged by thinking that the Church has no laws on the book that can be used to counter this behavior. Nor should they think that the Church has no power to adapt its legal system to meet this terrible conduct.

44. Should someone who blasphemes the name of God be excommunicated?

Someone who blasphemes the name of God commits a grave sin by violating the second commandment and should go to confession. It is not, however, an offense for which excommunication is imposed.

45. If one is ignorant that excommunication is the penalty for committing a certain act, is that person still excommunicated?

No, they are not. Canon 1324 states, among other things, that one who is unaware that a penalty for a certain act has been established cannot face the full penalty for the act. Thus, someone who might have otherwise faced excommunication for their deed is protected from the full penalty due to their ignorance that such a penalty is on the books. They might face interdict or some other penalty, but not excommunication.

46. Is a person who causes physical injury to a priest, bishop, or even the pope automatically excommunicated?

Each of these is actually a separate case. Is one excommunicated if one injures the pope? Yes. A bishop? No, but such an attacker is subject to *interdict* (c. 1332), a penalty which includes several but not all of the consequences of excommunication. A priest or religious? Again, no, but if the attack was motivated by hatred for the Church or the faith, such an attacker might face "a just penalty" (that is, one tailored to fit the specifics of the crime). All of these scenarios are discussed in canon 1370.

In this answer, we are assuming that this injury was caused deliberately, and by someone who is subject to excommunication, i.e., a Catholic. For example, the assassination attempt against Pope John Paul II in 1981 was committed by a Muslim, and hence by one not subject to ecclesiastical sanctions.

47. What if someone unjustly ruins the good reputation of a priest or bishop?

The Church takes an individual's right to a good reputation very seriously. While the Church is first to admit that it is made up of sinners, it is fundamental that the reputations of those involved in its mission critical to its credibility in the world. Thus, for example, canon 220 states that "no one is permitted to harm illegitimately the good reputation that a person possesses." Moreover, canon 128 states in part that "any one who illegitimately inflicts damages on another by an act placed with malice or negligence is obliged to repair the damage done." Other canons (such as cc. 221 and 1491) require ecclesiastical tribunals to adjudicate such cases when properly filed, and such cases are heard, though they are not common.

Notice a few things. First, the right to protect one's reputation is not just limited to priests and bishops— it extends to everyone in the Church. In certain circumstances, damaging the reputation of a priest may be more serious than damaging that of a lay person, but both clergy and laity alike enjoy protection of their reputation under canon law. Second, the right to a good reputation is not absolute. This right must yield in the face of legitimate actions taken that might indeed weaken one's reputation.

Even if an individual is facing penal action in the Church, the investigation that leads up to such prosecution must be conducted with an eye toward protecting the reputations of those involved (cc. 1717, 1719). That means, among other things, that the accused must not be labeled guilty before trial, and the innocent must not be embroiled unnecessarily.

While damaging another's reputation can be seriously sinful, and while some form of restitution or retraction might well be ordered, the action itself is not directly punishable by excommunication. So persons committing such deeds would not face excommunication on that point alone.

48. If one advocates heretical views, must one's heresy be "public" to incur excommunication? Or does the mere "private heresy" suffice for a "private excommunication"?

Your questions raise a couple of points. First, there is no such thing as "private" excommunication. At most, there is "automatic" excommunication, which could conceivably take place with few people knowing about it. But this does not make it "private"; it is simply not widely publicized. More importantly, though, canon 1330 states that an offense related to "will, doctrine, or knowledge" is not considered committed if no is aware of it. As far as canon law is concerned, there is no such thing as "private heresy," and one would not, for example, have to "turn one's self in" for holding heretical views. Nonetheless, harboring heretical or evil thoughts or intentions is sinful, and they need to be repented of and brought to confession. But it is not a situation that calls for the external exercise of Church authority that is invoked in ecclesiastical criminal cases.

49. Since excommunication is under the spiritual power and discernment of the Holy See and the bishops, should lay groups and individual Catholics petition for it to be used more frequently?

The question is a little bit like asking, "Since enforcement of the law is a police responsibility, should citizens lobby for its enforcement against criminals?" Provided one is motivated by a love for persons and a respect for justice, citizens of the state and Catholics in the Church may certainly express their views on the best way of going about upholding civil or canon law, including calling for its more rigorous enforcement. In fact, canon law itself recognizes in broad terms the right of Catholics "to make known their opinions on matters affecting the good of the Church" (c. 212).

Catholics making these suggestions should approach excommunication in the same way the Church approaches it, by recognizing it as a grave penalty, but one whose very existence is designed to bring about the reform of the individual.

50. How can I petition my bishop regarding the excommunication of pro-choice politicians?

A typed, one-page letter, signed with an address for reply, is an appropriate way to express one's views to your local bishop on this issue. (Emails tend to get noticed much less and phone calls usually accomplish little.)

It is not necessary to use "official-sounding" language or make long arguments in your letter. Bishops and their staff know what you are trying to say. Expect the courtesy of a reply, even if it is a non-committal one! If you don't receive an answer after a few weeks, write again. If two letters go unacknowledged, however, you may write to the papal nuncio and include copies of your earlier letters to the bishop. It would not be uncommon for the nuncio to redirect the letter to the bishop of the diocese from where it came, with a short cover note saying "for the attention it deserves." This is a way of giving the local bishop a chance to deal with the situation, but at the same time, it lets the bishop know that the nuncio is aware of the situation. Here is the nuncio's address: Papal Nuncio to the United States of America, His Excellency, Archbishop Pietro Sambi, 3339 Massachusetts Avenue NW, Washington, DC 20008.

Of course, you can always write directly to the Vatican. I have seen some amazingly direct answers to such "out of the blue" letters, but usually there is no direct response. But this does not mean your letter accomplished nothing. It just means the good done will not be evident to you. In general, though, the Vatican, like any good government, prefers to let local authorities to deal with the situation before the head office becomes involved.

Finally, remember that bishops and nuncios get letters from kooks and crazies all the time. Make sure you don't come off as just one more, making dramatic demands and insisting on impossible deadlines. Present yourself instead as a sincere Catholic motivated by charity and concerned for good order in the Church.

51. Why does the Church single-out abortion as meriting excommunication?

Actually, the Church *doesn't* single-out abortion as meriting excommunication. There are at least eight things (depending on how you count them) that today directly merit excommunication, abortion being just one of them.

The better question to ask is why the Church has retained abortion on its short list of excommunicable offenses (see question 13) in the first place. After all, there are many other very serious offenses being committed by Catholics that are not listed as punishable by excommunication, including other forms of homicide. So why did the Church keep abortion on the excommunication list?

Probably because the Church recognized that civil governments throughout the world had already abandoned pre-born babies to the selfish fury of abortionists and the whims of a selfish culture. Keeping abortion among the list of offenses punishable by excommunication is the Church's way of saying, "If civil governments are going to fail in their duty to protect the pre-born, we at least will do what we can to uphold their dignity and rights." We should be proud that our Church is defending the rights of the unborn.

52. How does denial of communion differ from full-fledged excommunication?

Denial of holy communion (i.e., the Eucharist) is quite distinct from excommunication, but both practices are receiving increased attention in Catholic life today and many people are confused about the differences between these two situations.

Excommunication is an ecclesiastical penalty. It is imposed or declared on those who have committed a certain type of canonical crime. In most cases, specific procedures have to be followed for the effects of excommunication to be fully visited upon an individual, and these steps include numerous procedural safeguards to guard against unjust infliction of such a severe penalty. To be sure, one of the consequences of excommunication is the loss of the right to the receive holy communion, but it is only one of the consequences that accompanies excommunication (for the others, see question 24). Finally, an excommunicated individual has to follow, in most cases, certain formal steps to have the penalty lifted.

On the other hand, denial of the Eucharist under canon 915 is not an ecclesiastical penalty but a sacramental disciplinary norm. It is designed to prevent the immediate harm that can be caused by the reception of the Eucharist by those whose own actions have demonstrated a fundamental disregard for the teachings of the Church. Because denial of the Eucharist is *not* a penalty, it is not limited to those cases in which one has been convicted of canonical crime. Canon 915 allows the Church to respond more quickly in the face of public sin. The other consequences that accompany excommunication (for example, restrictions on receiving the other sacraments or holding ecclesiastical office) are not included in a notice under canon 915 that one is not permitted to receive the Eucharist. Moreover, if one wishes to be readmitted to the Eucharist, instead of having to follow a detailed canonical procedure for the lifting of a penalty, one can simply repent of the sinful behavior, go to confession, and promise not to engage in it again.

53. Doesn't St. Paul speak about receiving the Eucharist worthily? Would that fit in here?

Yes. The passage of St. Paul to which you are referring is 1 Corinthians 11:27-29: "Whoever, therefore, eats the bread or drinks the cup of the Lord in an unworthy manner will be guilty of profaning the body and blood of the Lord. Let a man examine himself, and so eat of the bread and drink of the cup. For any one who eats and drinks without discerning the body eats and drinks judgment upon himself." This is a sobering statement for all Catholics to consider when approaching the altar of God to receive the Holy Eucharist.

Remember—it is God's grace that makes us worthy to receive the Eucharist. Yet, as Catholic moral teaching makes very clear, we must be in the state of grace in order to receive the Eucharist. We need to be "right" with God. Put another way, we need to be free of mortal sin—that is, we have avoided any action that fulfills the following three requirements: 1) it is gravely sinful in itself; 2) we committed it with sufficient awareness of its wrongness; and 3) we acted with sufficient freedom in choosing it. Only then should we approach the Eucharist.

54. Can or should canon law be changed to automatically excommunicate "pro-choice" Catholics, particularly politicians and members of advocacy groups like Catholics for a Free Choice?

Ecclesiastical penal law can be changed at any time by the pope, who can simply order such a change in the 1983 Code. He has done it before, adding new text to two canons (i.e., to c. 750 on the teaching office and c. 1371 on penal law). Though he is likely to consult with canonical advisors before acting, the pope does not need anyone's approval before making such changes. No Church body (e.g., the College of Cardinals) or official can authorize or prevent changes to the Code of Canon Law.

Moreover, let's not forget that many people directly involved in abortions, especially abortionist-physicians and their immediate assistants, already come with in the terms of canon 1398 on abortion or canon 1329 on accomplices.

Diocesan bishops can also enact new norms on Church penal discipline that are effective within their own dioceses (cc. 1315–1318). These diocesan laws would not be changes to the *Code of Canon Law* itself, of course. Most observers agree, though, that it is not easy for bishops to enact new penal law. Some canonists think that restrictions on episcopal authority in this area are too severe and should be relaxed somewhat to facilitate bishops' ability to react to local problems more quickly.

Beyond that, some officials in the Church can take quasi-penal action against individuals under certain circumstances (c. 1319), and there is some authority among bishops to stiffen penalties for crimes that are already treated in the *Code of Canon Law* (c. 1315). And as for those who engage in public advocacy of abortion, they might already face canonical sanction under canon 1369 (discussed in questions 42 and 43).

As to whether the Church *should* enact stricter penal laws—which would clearly allow bishops to excommunicate "pro-choice" Catholic politicians and public figures—that would depend on its assessment of the ability of present penal law to address the situation adequately, the difficulty of drafting new penal laws with sufficient exactitude, and the likelihood that it will achieve its effect without too many harmful side effects. Certainly, the Church has adapted her disciplinary law in the past to accommodate new situations, and it will doubtless do so in the future.

55. Why might stronger measures needed on the part of the Church against "pro-choice" Catholic politicians?

Because millions of innocent babies are being killed every year with the active support of some elected Catholics officials who are in a position to do something about it. This is a grave scandal, both for our Church and our world.

While Catholic politicians may argue that they are public servants and, as such, must represent the "diverse views of their constituents"—some of whom may be "pro-choice"—such an argument misses the point entirely. Such "inclusivity" might be OK when deciding where to put a superhighway or discussing the merits of raising (or lowering) taxes, but it is unacceptable when we are talking about objective moral truths. No one, for example, would argue that politicians should be "open" to a variety of views on murder—and, make no mistake, homicide is what we are talking about in regard to abortion.

When Catholic elected officials fail to support acceptable measures that protect the pre-born, a disastrous ripple effect spreads through our society—the erosion of its moral fiber spreads steadily and the "culture of death" (spoken of so poignantly by Pope John Paul II in his encyclical letter *Evangelium Vitae*, "the Gospel of Life") takes firmer hold. The long-standing and irresponsible conduct of pro-abortion Catholic politicians must be responded to by the Church's leaders in the clearest possible terms.

56. Isn't the Church being inconsistent when it automatically excommunicates those who procure abortions but does not excommunicate those who fight for "abortion rights"?

While *advocating* deliberate death for innocent human beings is a grave evil, actually *imposing* this type of death on them is even worse. On the other hand, as the answer to question 45 makes clear, there are actually a number of factors that might well mitigate incurring excommunication by at least some of those directly involved in abortion, defenses that clearly would *not* apply to those advocating for it. Finally, the Church might well decide one day that advocacy of abortion *is* such a serious offense that it should be met with excommunication, so the question might be obviated.

57. Don't Catholic politicians have the responsibility to uphold the laws of the land, regardless of whether those laws go against their Catholic beliefs?

Legislative politicians—members of Congress and state legislators, for example—don't uphold the law of the land; they make it. And in making public policy, political leaders should use their great, entrusted powers to serve all persons, most especially those who can't protect themselves. Moreover, no political system is at liberty to disregard natural law and the fundamental rights of persons. Those political leaders who have done so rank among the worst despots in human history. The Catholic Church allows wide discretion to civil leaders—and to Catholics acting in the civil arena—to shape their societies as they think best (cc. 209, 225, 227). But where their actions result in things such as the execution of the innocent, the Church can, will, and must speak out (c. 747).

Any fair reading of American history will show that Catholics have never been slow to sacrifice for the common good of this nation. Catholic politicians in particular, because they belong to a Church with 2,000 years of experience in trying to shape societies according to the salvific teachings of Christ, should know better than to think that they are serving any interests but evil ones by abandoning pre-born babies to abortionist propaganda and greed.

Certainly, too, it should be recalled that American bishops have used ecclesiastical sanctions, even excommunication, against Catholics who tried to thwart the legitimate recognition of civil rights (e.g., the 1962 excommunication of a notorious racist in New Orleans). Interestingly, some of the same voices who would have cheered stiff ecclesiastical penalties in pursuit of racial equality are among those now telling bishops to stay out of politics when it comes to pro-life witness.

58. Isn't the judgment of one's individual conscience the most important factor for public figures to consider in these matters?

Be very careful here. There is a great deal of confusion today as to the nature of individual conscience. Some of this confusion is the result of simple ignorance and poor instruction; to a large degree, though, it is due to the attempts of some people to spread the notion that individual conscience alone can decide whether an act is moral or immoral. This is a dangerous error.

Individuals are not the ultimate arbiters of right and wrong. Instead, all responsible people must form their consciences according to the requirements of natural law. Christians, moreover, must adhere to the teachings of Christ and His Church. One is not free, for example, to treat the Eucharist with disdain because one thinks it is only symbol, and one cannot lie on tax returns because the "the government has no right to take my money." In general, one cannot pick and choose among the rules and laws that govern our life, deciding on a case by case basis which ones deserve our cooperation and which ones do not. Properly understood, conscience is the *application* of the objective moral law to a particular situation; it does not *create* the moral law out of thin air.

This is an entirely separate case from the relatively rare circumstances in which following a certain law might itself be immoral, and, on this basis, one chooses to disobey the law as a matter of conscience. Generally, though, one's disagreement with a law is not a sufficient basis for disobeying it. Moreover, inconvenience is not grounds to ignore the law. In fact, sometimes legal and moral principles require us to act, even though we as citizens or as Christians might face persecution for adhering to these principles or the teachings of the Church.

59. Some have said that excommunicating politicians who defy Church teaching would make them "martyrs" for their beliefs. Could you comment on this?

To some degree, the "creation of a martyr" problem is raised any time an organization with authority takes action against an individual member. But keep in mind—excommunication is meant to bring about the personal reform of the individual, and the Church should not be slow to use the means intended to work that salvific end. Moreover, it is not true that every excommunicate becomes a martyr to the cause. To the contrary, a clear statement by the Church that the actions that led to the excommunication were inconsistent with Catholic belief or practice causes some excommunicants to lose their followers. Excommunication often has the effect of making people decide, in quite stark terms, which way they want to go—the Church's way, or theirs. Finally, if the offender repents of his actions, his reconciliation is itself a powerful testimony to those who might have been misled by the earlier poor example. From evil, good can flow even more abundantly.

60. Because excommunication is an ecclesial punishment, it is generally seen in a negative light. Is there a "positive" side to excommunication? What, if any, are its good fruits?

Well, in a variety of ways, we have seen that excommunication has the same place in society that any form of just punishment has. We have seen how the Church is slow to inflict excommunication, and discussed the many safeguards that are in place to prevent its being used inappropriately. Most of all, we have seen the primary purpose behind excommunication is the personal reform of the offender. When excommunication works, it honors all these ends and accomplishes all these goals. When it does not work, it is probably the result of the individual's hardening of the heart against the grace of conversion that, more than anything else, the Church wishes to accomplish.

Glossary of Terms

Anathema: A Greek term; refers to excommunication from the Church, promulgated solemnly by the pope; the term is not currently used.

Annulment: A common term for what is more accurately called a *declaration of matrimonial nullity,* an official declaration that what appeared to be a valid marriage was not one. Not a divorce.

Apostasy: The deliberate, post-baptismal rejection of the Christian faith.

Canon: A specific, numbered provision of canon law.

Canon Law: The one-volume book which contains the complete text of the 1,752 individual canons of Church law. Most recently issued for Roman Catholics in 1983.

Censure: An ecclesiastical penalty by which a Catholic is deprived of certain spiritual goods as a result of some wrong-doing; designed to bring about personal repentance and reform in an individual.

Declaration of Nullity: Also, *declaration of matrimonial nullity* or *annulment.* The decision by a diocesan tribunal or other qualified canonical court that what appeared to be, from one or more points of view, a valid marriage, was not one.

Denial of Holy Communion: the loss of the right to receive the Holy Eucharist in the Catholic Church; canon 915 permits competent ecclesiastical authorities (usually the diocesan bishop) to deny communion to Catholics under certain conditions.

Eastern Catholics: those members of the Catholic Church who, while remaining in full communion with Rome, belong to Churches *sui iuris* other than Latin Church, and who follow a liturgical rite other than the Roman rite. Examples include Maronite, Chaldean, and Melkite rites. Eastern Churches are governed by their own code of canon law, issued in 1990.

Excommunication: a term meaning, literally, "out of communion." The most severe ecclesiastical penalty the Church can impose on its members for certain offenses; must follow certain procedures.

Expiatory Penalty: An ecclesiastical penalty; intended to maintain good order in the Church and satisfy the demands of justice.

Ferendae Sententiae: A type of penalty that is imposed by the judgment of a court or by the decree of a superior, when a person has been found guilty of a canonical offence; a penalty imposed after a *formal process*, either administrative or judicial.

Heresy: The obstinate doubt or denial by a baptized person of a truth that must be believed with divine and Catholic faith, as described in canon 751 of the 1983 Code.

Interdict: A type of censure by which the faithful, while remaining in communion with the Church, are forbidden the use of certain sacred things, such as liturgical services, some of the sacraments, and Christian burial; imposed by competent ecclesiastical authority, usually either the local bishop or the Holy See.

Latae Sententiae: A type of penalty that one incurs *automatically* by committing an offence, without it being formally imposed or declared; the number of offenses for which one can be automatically excommunicated is quite limited under the 1983 Code of Canon Law.

Ministerial Participation: functioning in a ministerial role in liturgical or sacramental celebrations—for a priest, this would include celebrating Mass or the sacraments; for a layperson, this would include serving as a lector, an extraordinary minister of the Eucharist, usher, etc.; prohibited to those who have been excommunicated.

Natural Law: the rational participation in the eternal law of God; not to be confused with the "laws of nature" (such as the "laws" of physics); knowable by human reason without recourse to divine revelation.

Reserved Offenses: ecclesiastical penalties that can only be lifted or removed by higher Church authority, usually the Apostolic See (i.e., the pope); carefully stipulated in canon law; e.g., desecration of the Eucharist, physically assaulting the pope, consecration of a bishop without a papal mandate.

Sacramental Seal: the requirement, binding under pain of excommunication, that a confessor not disclose, directly or equivalently, the identity of a penitent and the sins confessed.

Schism: literally, "to split"; the refusal of submission to the Roman Pontiff or refusing to join in communion with the Churches subject to him.

Suspension: a censure by which a cleric (i.e., a bishop, priest, or deacon) is deprived, entirely or partially, of the use of the power of holy orders by competent ecclesiastical authority.

Tolerati: literally, "tolerated ones"; formerly, the lesser of the two degrees of excommunication; the term is no longer used.

Vitandi: literally, "ones to be avoided"; in older canon law, the more serious of the two types of excommunication, by which the faithful were to avoid even contact with the excommunicated person; not found in the 1983 Code.

Index

Topic/Question No(s).

Abortion, 13, 42, 43, 51, 54-56
   as an excommunicable
     offense, 51
   promotion of the "right" to,
     56
Absolution,
   attempted by a deacon or
     lay person, 40
   of an accomplice, 13
Acta Apostolicae Sedis, 29
Amish, 20, 28
Annulment, 14
Aparicio, Bishop, 32
Apostasy, 13
Appeal, right of, 30
Baltimore, Third Plenary
   Council of, 14
Becket, Thomas à, 32
Benedict XV, Pope, 3
Bible, 21, 22
   support for excommunica-
     tion, 21
Bishop,
   consecration of without
     papal mandate, 19
Blasphemy, 44
Buddhist monasticism, 20
Canon law,
   1917 Code, 3
   1983 Code, 3
   as a model of fairness, 30
   definition of, 2
   history of, 3

Topic/Question No(s).

*Catechism of the Catholic
   Church*, 36
Censures, 11, 17
Church, the
   authority to excommunicate,
     22
   full communion with, 5
Churches *sui iuris*, 37
Civil law, 6, 30
Commandment, the Second, 44
Conclave, 13
Confession, seal of, 13
   authority of confessors, 17
Congregationalist churches, 20
Conscience, individual, 58
Corpus Christi, 32
Declaration of nullity, *see
   Annulment*
Divine law, 2
Divorce and remarriage, 3, 14
Eastern Catholics, 2, 12, 37
Ecclesiastical penalties, 1, 6, 11
   types of, 11
Ecumenical council, 3, 8
England, Church of, 20, 32
Eucharist,
   denial of, 43, 52
   desecration of, 19, 41
   worthy reception of, 53
   ministerial participation in,
     24
   worthy reception of, 53
Euthanasia, 39
Expiatory penalties, 11, 17

Topic/Question No(s).

Excommunication,
    administrative vs. judicial,
        12
    authority of, 18
    definition of, 1, 4
    history of, 10
    lobbying for more extensive
        use of, 50
    "major" vs. "minor," 16
    necessity of, 9
    offense against charity, 17
    offenses for which one can
        incur, 12
    practical effects of, 24
    process of, 12
    role in Church history, 32
    spiritual effects of, 25
    "types" of, 15
    universal character of, 31
    use in other religions, 20
Fathers, Church, 3
Ferendae sententiae, 12
Gracida, Bishop Rene, 32
Gratian, 3
Gregory VII, Pope, 32
Gregory VIII, Pope, 3
Hell, 23
Henry VIII, King, 32
Heresy, 13, 48
    "private" vs. "public," 48
Infallibility, papal, 33
Interdict, 24, 40, 46
Inter mirifica, 42
Jews,
    excommunication of, 6
    practice of excommunica-
        tion, 20
John XXIII, Pope, 3
John Paul II, Pope, 3

Topic/Question No(s).

Latae sententiae, 12
L'Osservatore Romano, 29
Lumen Gentium, 5
Luther, Martin, 32
Maronite Catholics, 2
Media, the, 42
Melkite rite, 37
Mennonites, 28
Middle Ages, 3
Moral law, unchangeable charac-
    ter of, 15
Mormons, 20
Muslims,
    excommunication of, 6
Natural law, 2, 6
    definition of, 8
New Testament, 3, 21, 22
Nicea, Council of, 3
Orthodox churches, 37
Paul, St., 21, 53
Perez, Leander, 32
Politicians, Catholic, 42, 43, 50,
    54, 55, 56, 57
    support for abortion, 54, 55,
        56
    excommunication of, 50, 54,
        59
Pope, physical assault on, 13,
    19, 46
Priests, 46, 47
Protestants, excommunication
    of, 6
Reconciliation, 19
Reformation, Protestant, 3, 20,
    32
Reserved offenses, 19
Roman Empire, 3
Roman law, 3
Rummelt, Archbishop Joseph, 32

Topic/Question No(s).

Sacramentals, 24
Sacraments, celebration of, 24
Schism, 13
Shunning, 28
Sin, grave, 8, 27
Suspension, 24, 40
Tolerati, 16, 28
Trent, Council of, 3
Tribunal, 30
Vatican I, 3
Vatican II, 3, 5, 8
Vitandi, 16, 28
World War II, 7

Index of Canons Cited

Canon No.	Question No(s).
18	12
112	37
128	47
205	4, 5
209	57
212	49
220	47
221	30, 47
225	57
227	57
331	18
336	33
337	18
360	18
381	18
747	57
750	54
915	14, 43, 52
1312	17
1313	14
1314	12
1315	54
1316	54
1317	54
1318	54
1319	54
1321	12
1322	12
1323	12
1324	12, 45
1326	40
1329	54
1330	48

Canon No.	Question No(s).
1331	12, 16, 24, 27
1332	24, 46
1333	24
1336	17
1341	12
1353	30
1354	19
1355	19
1356	19
1357	19
1358	17
1364	13
1367	13, 19, 41
1369	42, 43, 54
1370	13, 33, 46
1371	54
1378	13, 40
1379	40
1382	13, 33
1388	13
1393	39
1397	39
1398	13, 42, 43, 54
1399	39
1401	18
1404	33
1405	18
1412	30
1421	30
1425	12, 18
1448	30
1477	30
1481	30
1491	47
1501	30
1547	30
1717	47
1719	47
1723	30
1725	30
1727	30

About the Author

Dr. Edward N. Peters received his civil law degree from the University of Missouri at Columbia and his doctoral degree in canon law from The Catholic University of America. He has held a number of canonical administrative posts, including that of diocesan vice-chancellor and chancellor, director of canonical affairs, defender of the bond, and collegial judge in diocesan and appellate tribunals. He is the author of several scholarly and popular books on canon law, and his articles and reviews have appeared in over 50 publications. He maintains a prominent website devoted to canon law, www.canonlaw.info. Dr. Peters currently holds the Edmund Cardinal Szoka Chair at Sacred Heart Major Seminary in Detroit and is a consultant to several ecclesiastical institutions and persons.